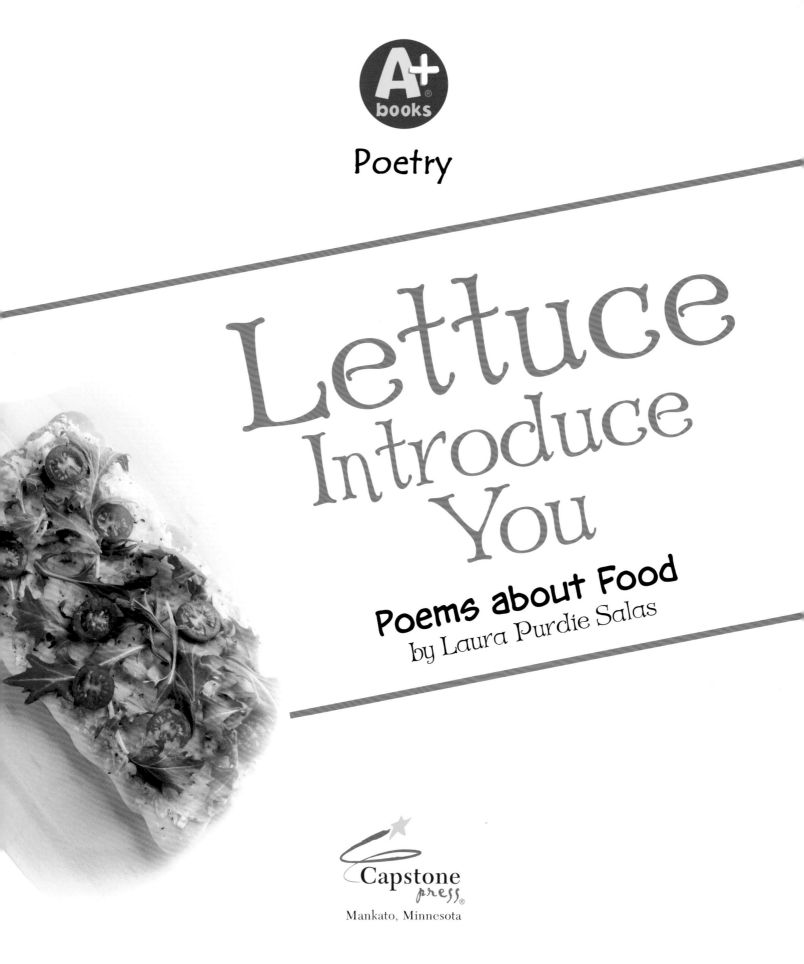

Poetry

Lettuce Introduce You

Poems about Food
by Laura Purdie Salas

Capstone
press®
Mankato, Minnesota

An Inviting Salad

Tomato, have you met the greens?

Lettuce introduce you!

Carrots, you look fabulous —

That color really suits you.

I hope you're here to mix things up

I hope you're feeling hearty

'Cause now that we've all gathered here

It's time to throw this party!

How Do You Like Your Milk?

Milk is gulped or swallowed,
It's flavored, stirred, and tasted
Mom says milk should be drunk up
and never, ever wasted

Milk is chugged or guzzled,
It's slurped or burped or sipped
But milk is always extra good
on cookies that are dipped

Fresh
POP-CORN

each
kernel

POPS

with a
bubblewrap
burst

sweet
buttery
corn-juice

slides
down

my
throat

Definition of
Carrots

Crammed with vitamin

A, you see, these

Roots grow in

Rows of

Orange underground, with

Tops sprouting

Soft leafy green overhead

Can't Spaghetti-nough!

noodles

slippery, white

sliding, twirling, dangling

Parmesan, butter, garlic, meatballs

rolling, splashing, staining

messy, red

sauce

How Fish Becomes Sushi

There once was a ruby-red snapper

With shimmering scales quite dapper

It gazed at the bait

Thought, "Yum, that looks great" —

Now the snapper's inside a grass wrapper

Snapper is a fish used in sushi. It is wrapped with vinegared rice in a seaweed wrapper.

Sweet NOthing

Sugary, see-through, crispy glaze, a tasty gift wrap for a donut

Pillowy perfect inside dissolves on my eager tongue

But here is my favorite part: the empty center circle

Green

and round

and wrapped in leaves

I try to shove them up my sleeves

I'm sure they're very good for me

But tasty?

I do not agree!

They look

like little

lettuce heads

So there's a part of me that dreads

Forcing leaf balls down my throat

Order pizza —

That's my vote!

Leafy Marbles in My Mouth

Brussels sprouts are a vegetable that look like small lettuce heads.

Pizza in Motion

Pizza making must be fun

Knead and pound, the dough is done

Make a whipping, spinning toss

Splash on tons of pizza sauce

Add sausage and some bacon, please

And extra, extra, extra cheese!

Making Pancakes

pour the batter
  Plip
  Plop

brown both sides
  Flip
  Flop

spread the butter
  Tip
  Top

let the syrup
  Drip
  Drop

eat them all up
  Don't
  Stop!

I'll Spell It Out for You

Nothing
tastes better on
a blustery, W-E-T day
Nothing else warms my cold insides
like S-O-U-P!

Summer Rain

I bite into sweet

summer — it drips down my chin

Watermelon days

Skyscraper Sandwich

I once built a sandwich on rye

Swiss cheese and bologna stretched high

It stood straight and tall

I did not let it fall

I stopped when my sandwich hit sky!

Too Early!

Mom says to wake up

    I don't want to

It's the middle of the night

Right?

    Wrong

Dad makes me a

"Cheer up!" waffle-boy

with blueberry eyes and

a fresh citrus smile

    What's he so happy about?

graham cracker: flat as my wooden bench

oozy warm marshmallows, charred and crispy
on the outside, melty on the inside, puff out like squished balloons
and chocolate that melts faster than I can eat it
drips onto my fingers over the edges of the

graham cracker: handle for hot, campout heaven

S'Mores

The Language of Poetry

Couplet — two lines that end with words that rhyme

 **Repetition** — the use of a word or phrase more than one time

 **Rhyme** — to have an end sound that is the same as the end sound of another word

 **Rhythm** — the pattern of beats in a poem

Acrostic

The subject of the poem is written straight down the page. Each line of the poem starts with one letter of the word. "Definition of Carrots" (page 8) is an acrostic poem.

Concrete

A poem in which the words are shaped like the subject of the poem. "S'Mores" (page 26) is a concrete poem.

Free Verse

A poem that does not follow a set pattern or rhythm. It often does not rhyme. "Too Early" (page 25) is an example of free verse.

Haiku

A short poem that describes a scene in nature. It has five syllables in the first line, seven syllables in the second line, and five syllables in the third line. "Summer Rain" (page 20) is a haiku.

Limerick

A 5-line poem that follows a certain rhythm. The first, second, and fifth lines rhyme, and so do the third and fourth lines. "Skyscraper Sandwich" (page 22) is a limerick.

Glossary

blustery (BLUHSS-tuh-ree) — very windy

bologna (buh-LOH-nee) — a sandwich meat

bubble wrap (BUH-buhl RAP) — the plastic sheets used to protect items being shipped; the sheets are covered with small bubbles.

charred (CHARD) — slightly burned

chug (CHUHG) — to take big, fast drinks of something

cram (KRAM) — to fit things into a small space

dapper (DAP-uhr) — stylish

dissolve (di-ZOLV) — to disappear little by little until nothing is left

glaze (GLAYZ) — a thin, sweet coat of icing

gulp (GUHLP) — to swallow something quickly and noisily

hearty (HAR-tee) — enthusiastic or sincere

kernel (KUR-nuhl) — a grain or seed of corn

knead (NEED) — to press and fold dough many times

oozy (OO-zee) — very soft and somewhat runny

pillowy (PIL-oh-wee) — light and fluffy

rye (RYE) — a type of dark brown bread

snapper (SNAP-uhr) — a kind of fish

Read More

Freese, Susan M. *Carrots to Cupcakes: Reading, Writing, and Reciting Poems about Food.* Poetry Power. Edina, Minn.: Abdo, 2008.

Rock, Brian. *Don't Play with Your Food.* Chesterfield, Va.: First Light, 2004.

Internet Sites

FactHound offers a safe, fun way to find Internet sites related to this book. All of the sites on FactHound have been researched by our staff.

Here's how:

1. Visit *www.facthound.com*

2. Choose your grade level.

3. Type in this book ID **1429617039** for age-appropriate sites. You may also browse subjects by clicking on letters, or by clicking on pictures and words.

4. Click on the **Fetch It** button.

FactHound will fetch the best sites for you!

Index of Poems

Can't Spaghetti-nough, 9

Definition of Carrots, 8

Fresh Pop-Corn, 7

How Do You Like Your Milk?, 4

How Fish Becomes Sushi, 10

I'll Spell It Out for You, 19

Inviting Salad, An, 2

Leafy Marbles in My Mouth, 14

Making Pancakes, 18

Pizza in Motion, 17

Skyscraper Sandwich, 22

S'mores, 26

Summer Rain, 20

Sweet Nothing, 13

Too Early!, 25

A+ Books are published by Capstone Press,
151 Good Counsel Drive, P.O. Box 669, Mankato, Minnesota 56002.
www.capstonepress.com

1 2 3 4 5 6 13 12 11 10 09 08

Library of Congress Cataloging-in-Publication Data
Salas, Laura Purdie.
    Lettuce introduce you : poems about food / by Laura Purdie Salas.
    p. cm. — (A+ books. Poetry)
    Summary: "A collection of original, food-themed poetry for children accompanied by striking photos. The book demonstrates a variety of common poetic forms and defines poetic devices" — Provided by publisher.
    Includes bibliographical references and index.
    ISBN-13: 978-1-4296-1703-1 (hardcover)
    ISBN-10: 1-4296-1703-9 (hardcover)
    1. Food — Juvenile poetry. 2. Children's poetry, American. I. Title. II. Series.
PS3619.A4256L47 2008
811'.6 — dc22   2008003896

Credits
Jenny Marks, editor; Ted Williams, set designer; Renée T. Doyle, book designer; Wanda Winch, photo researcher; Sarah L. Schuette, photo stylist

Photo Credits
All photos by Capstone Press/Karon Dubke

Note to Parents, Teachers, and Librarians
Lettuce Introduce You: Poems about Food uses colorful photographs and a nonfiction format to introduce children to poetry. This book is designed to be read independently by an early reader or to be read aloud to a pre-reader. The images help early readers and listeners understand the poems and concepts discussed. The book encourages further learning by including the following sections: The Language of Poetry, Glossary, Read More, Internet Sites, and Index of Poems. Early readers may need assistance using these features.

Capstone Press thanks Pagliai's Pizza of Mankato, Minnesota, for assistance in making this book.